CELEBRATION SERIES®

THE PIANO ODYSSEY®

PIANO
REPERTOIRE

9

ISBN 0-88797-701-4

Celebration Series®

The Piano Odyssey®

The *Celebration Series®* was originally published in 1987 to international acclaim. In 1994, a second edition was released and received with heightened enthusiasm. Launched in 2001 and building on the success of previous editions, the *Celebration Series®, The Piano Odyssey®* takes advantage of the wealth of new repertoire and the changing interests and needs of teachers.

The series is breathtaking in its scope, presenting a true musical odyssey through the ages and their respective musical styles. The albums are graded from late elementary to early intermediate (albums Introductory to 3) through intermediate (albums 4 to 8) to advanced and concert repertoire (albums 9 and 10). Each volume of repertoire comprises a carefully selected grouping of pieces from the Baroque, Classical, Romantic, and 20th-century style periods. *Studies/Etudes* albums present compositions especially suited for building technique as well as musicality relevant to the repertoire of each level. *Student Workbooks* and recordings are available to assist in the study and enjoyment of the music. In addition, the comprehensive *Handbook for Teachers* is an invaluable pedagogical resource.

A Note on Editing and Performance Practice

Most Baroque and early Classical composers wrote few dynamics, articulation, or other performance indications in their scores. Interpretation was left up to the performer, with the expectation that the performance practice was understood. In this edition, therefore, most of the dynamics and tempo indications in the Baroque and early Classical pieces have been added by the editors. These editorial markings, including fingering and the execution of ornaments, are intended to be helpful rather than definitive.

The keyboard instruments of the 17th and early 18th centuries lacked the sustaining power of the modern piano. Consequently, the usual keyboard touch was detached rather than legato. The pianist should assume that a lightly detached touch is appropriate for Baroque and early Classical music, unless a different approach is indicated by the style of the music.

Even into the 19th century, composers' scores could vary from copy to copy or edition to edition. Thus, the editors of the *Celebration Series®* have also made editorial choices in much of the Classical and Romantic repertoire presented in the series.

This edition follows the policy that the bar line cancels accidentals. In accordance with current practice, cautionary accidentals are added only in cases of possible ambiguity.

Teachers and students should refer to the companion guides – the *Student Workbooks* and the *Handbook for Teachers* – for further discussion of style and pedagogical elements. For examination requirements of The Royal Conservatory of Music, please refer to the current *Piano Syllabus*.

Dr. Trish Sauerbrei
Editor-in-Chief

Contents

Sinfonia No. 6 in E Major

BWV 792

Johann Sebastian Bach
(1685 – 1750)

Source: *Clavierbüchlein vor Wilhelm Friedemann Bach (1720)*

19
23
27
31
35
38
(d)
(e)

Sinfonia No. 11 in G Minor

BWV 797

Johann Sebastian Bach
(1685 – 1750)

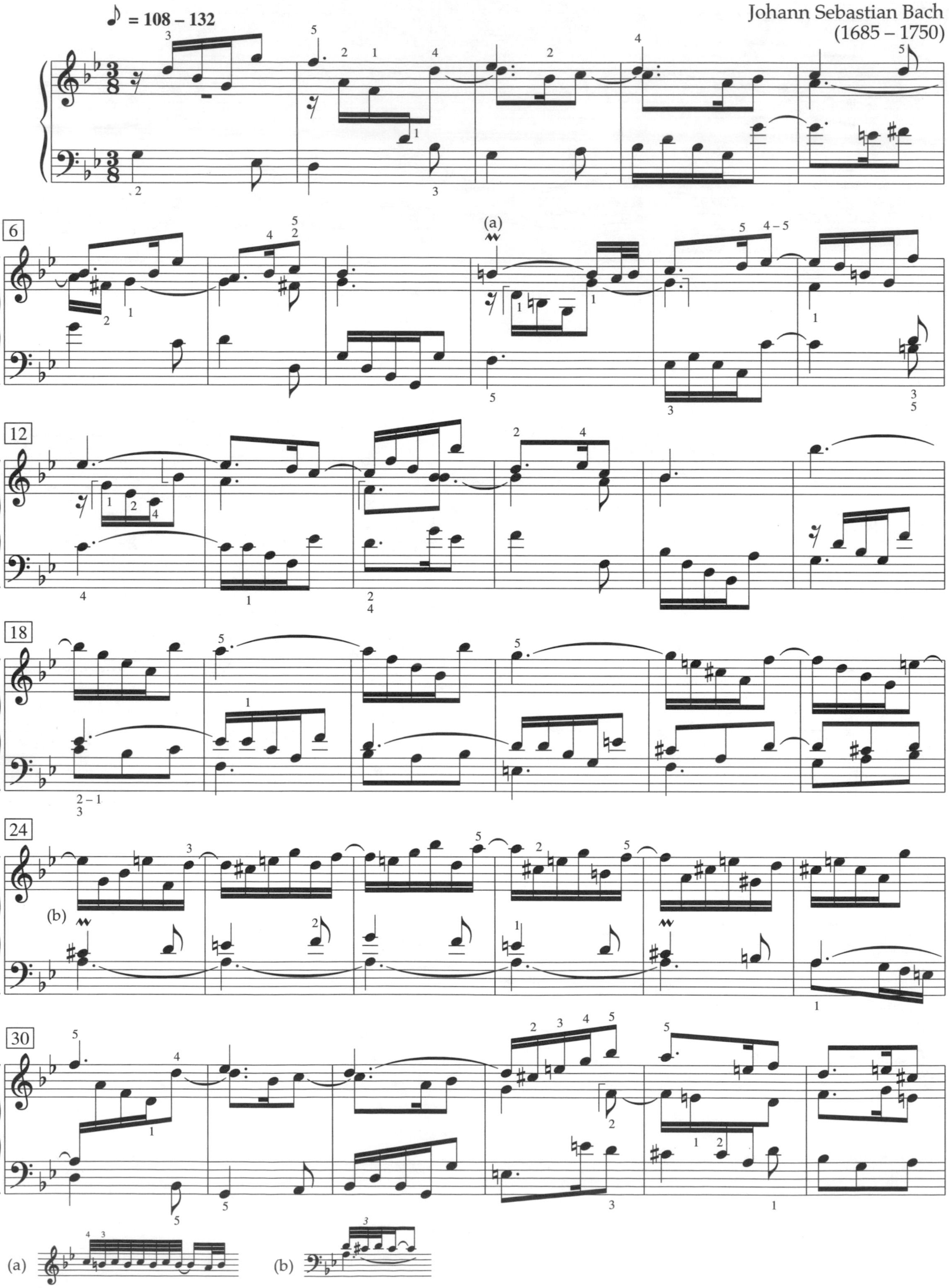

♪ = 108 – 132

(a)

(b)

Source: *Clavierbüchlein vor Wilhelm Friedmann Bach* (1720)

36
42
48
54
60
66

Sonata in C Major

L 104, K 159

Domenico Scarlatti
(1685 – 1757)

Most eighth notes should be played detached.
For examinations, any two of the three Scarlatti sonatas are to be played as one selection.

Source: *Pièces pour le clavecin* (1752)

Sonata in D Minor

L 413, K 9

Domenico Scarlatti
(1685 – 1757)

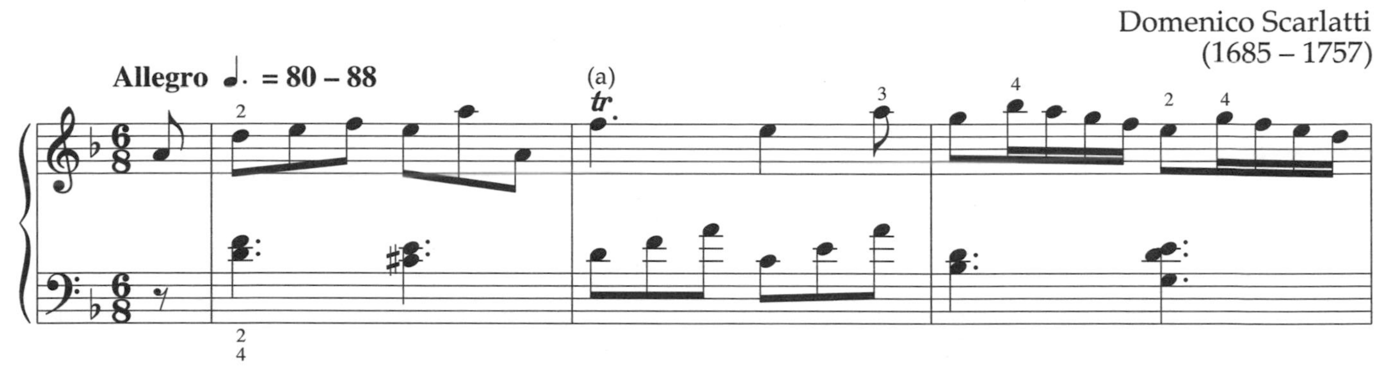

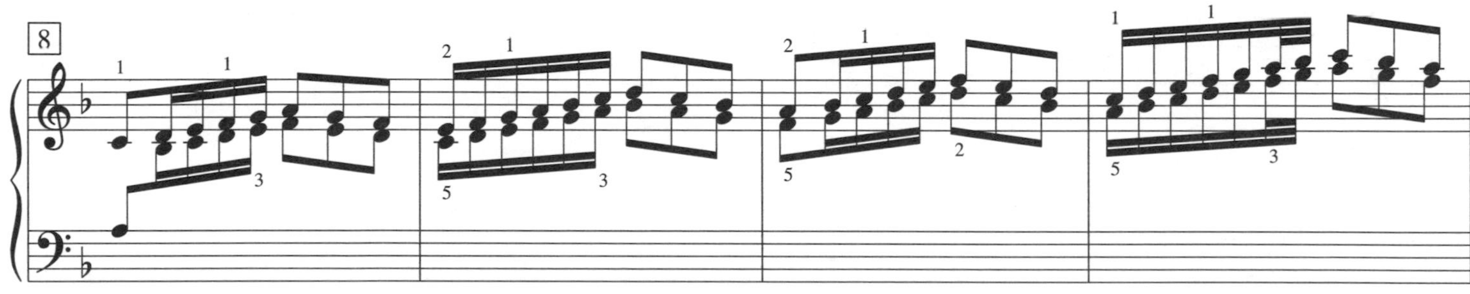

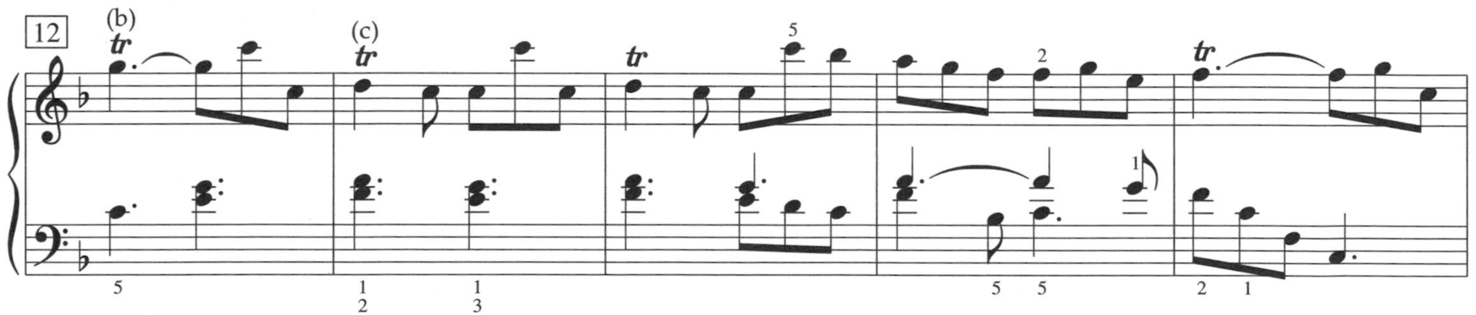

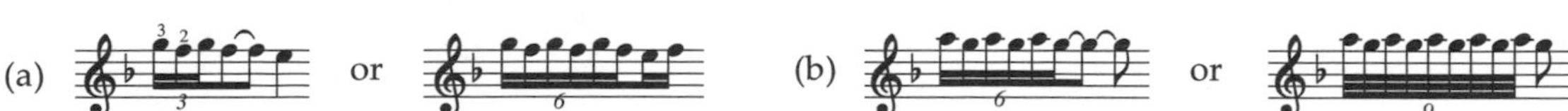

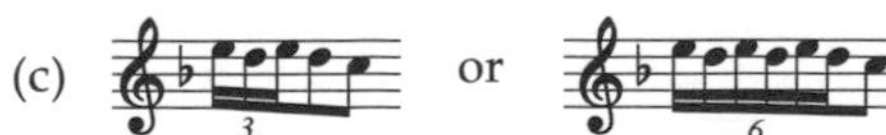

For examinations, any two of the three Scarlatti sonatas are to be played as one selection.

Source: *Essercizi* (no. 9) (1738)

17
22
27
31
36
(d)
(e)
(d)
(e)
or

* G in Longo edition

Sonata in D Major

L 463, K 430

Domenico Scarlatti
(1685 – 1757)

Non presto ma a tempo di ballo ♩. = 63 – 76

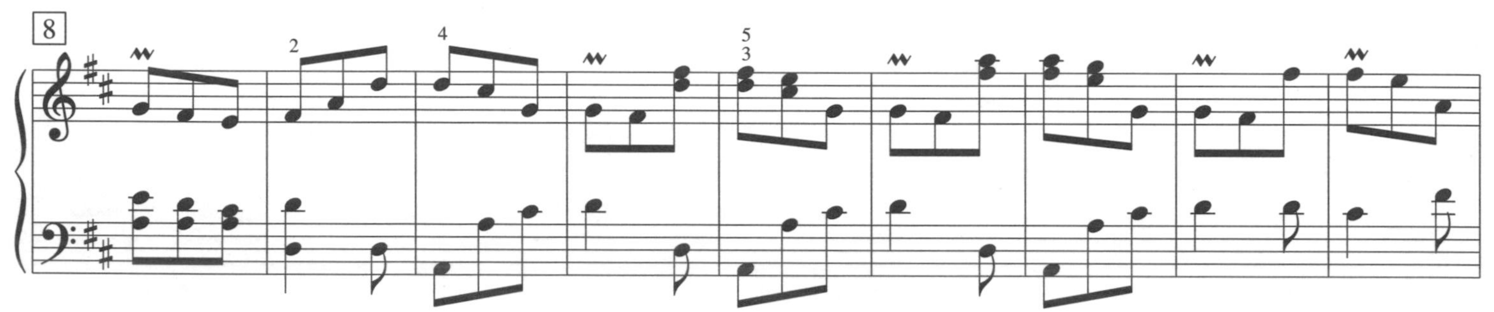

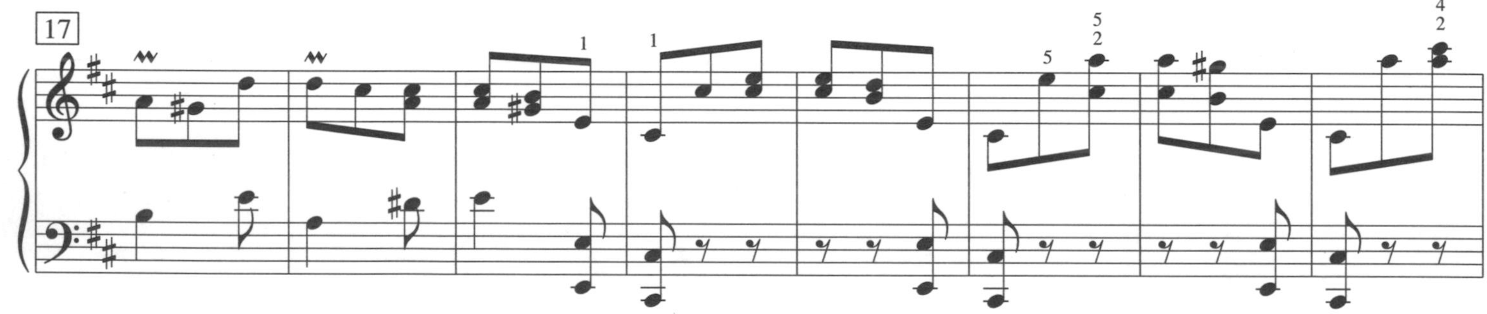

(a) 

For examinations, any two of the three Scarlatti sonatas are to be played as one selection.

32
40
(b)
47
55
62
(b)
or

69
77
85
93
101

Prelude and Fugue in C Minor

BWV 847

Praeludium

Johann Sebastian Bach
(1685 – 1750)

Source: *Das Wohltemperierte Clavier*, book 1 (1722)

11
14
17
20
22
24
f

26
28
Presto
30
32
34
Adagio
(a)
Allegro (Tempo I)
36
(a)

Fuga a 3

♩ = 80 – 84

The subject of the fugue may be played slightly detached, or with the following articulation:

Le coucou (Rondeau)

Louis-Claude Daquin
(1694 – 1772)

Most eighth notes should be played detached.

Source: *Premier livre de pièces de clavecin,* troisième suite (Paris, 1735)

1er Couplet

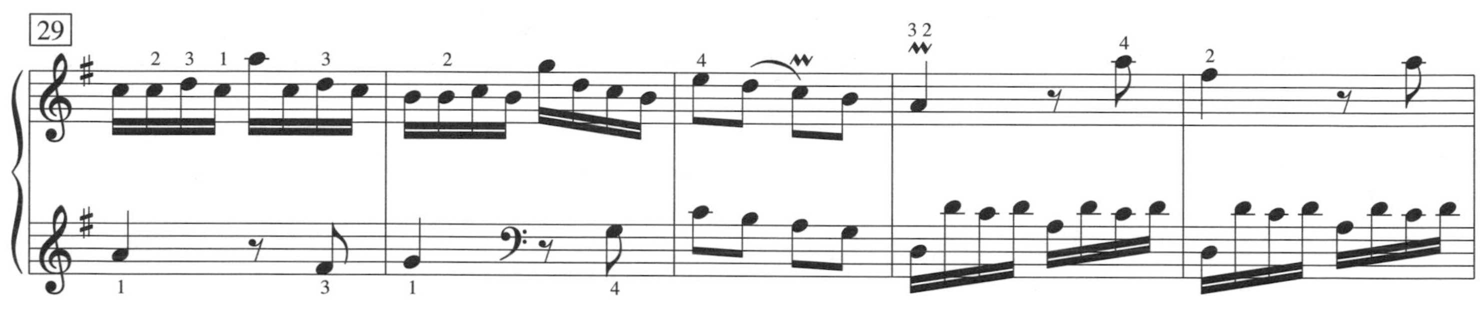

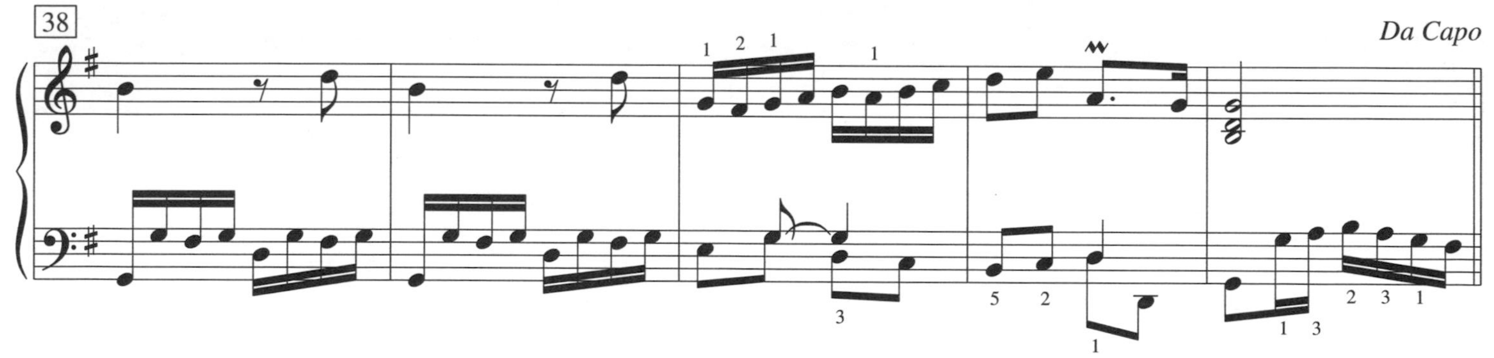

2^e Couplet

47

51

55
(e)

60

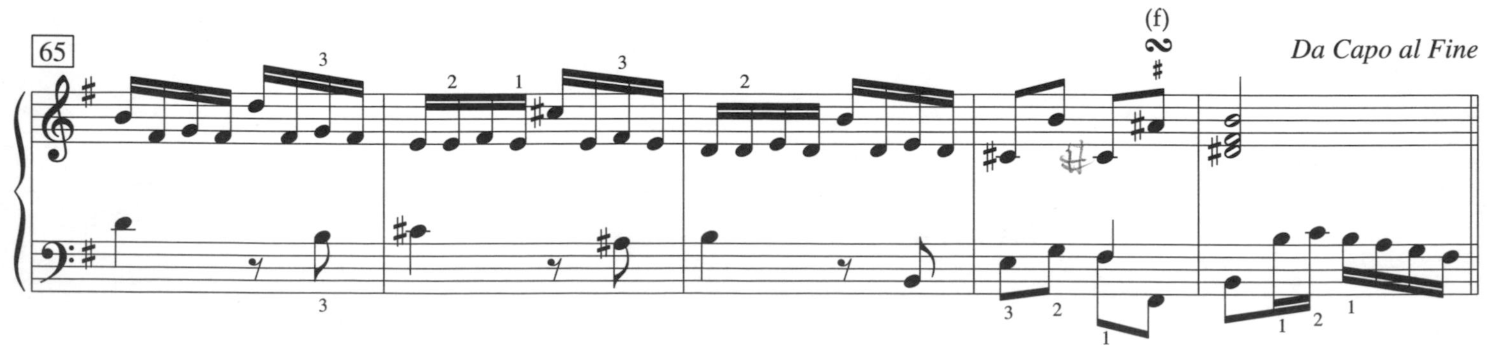
65
(f)
Da Capo al Fine

(e)
(f)

Sonata in C Minor

Wq 48/4, H 27

III

Carl Philipp Emanuel Bach
(1714 – 1788)

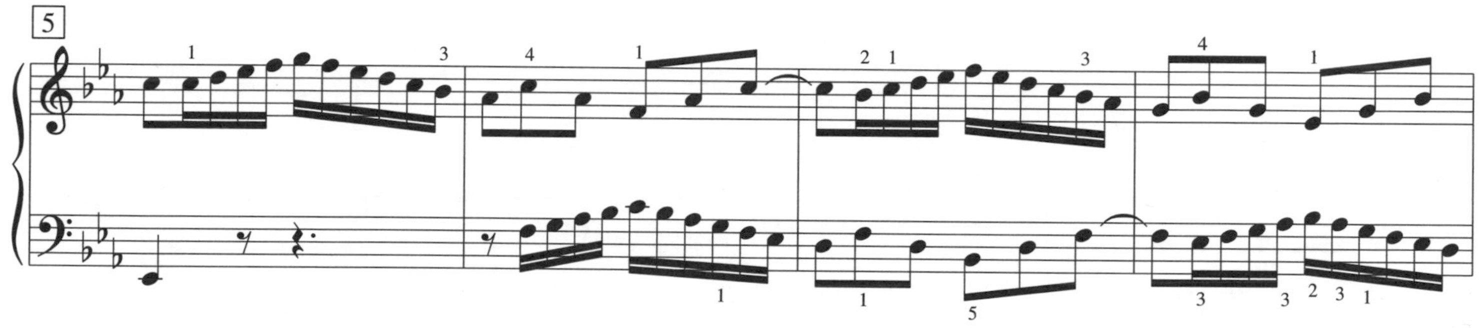

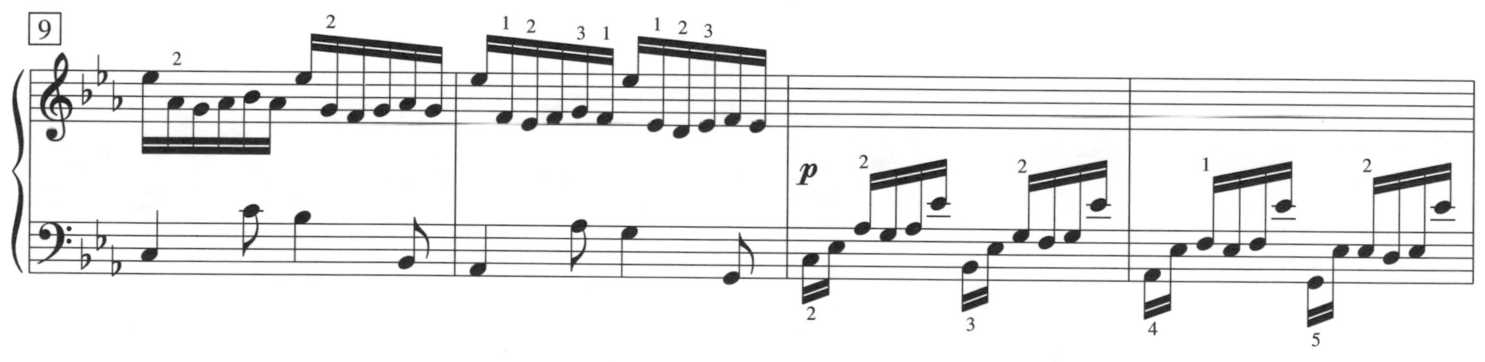

(a) 

Source: *Sei sonate per cembalo* (Prussian Sonatas) (Nuremburg, 1742)

17
tr
22
26
30
p
f
34

39
44
48
52
56
p
f

Fantasia in D Minor

K 397 (385g)

The stroke (ꜜ) indicates *staccato.*

Source: This work is a fragment, likely composed in 1782 in Vienna.

Presto
Adagio
cresc.
f
p

Presto
44
no pedal
Adagio
45
51
f
p
m.d.
m.s.
pedal
Allegretto ♩ = 104 – 112
54
dolce
63
1.
(a)

70
2.
75
80
86
no pedal
pedal
87
a tempo
rall.
p dolce
f
91
p
f
p
pp
100
f
ff

Sonata in C Major

K330 (300h)

II

Wolfgang Amadeus Mozart
(1756 – 1791)

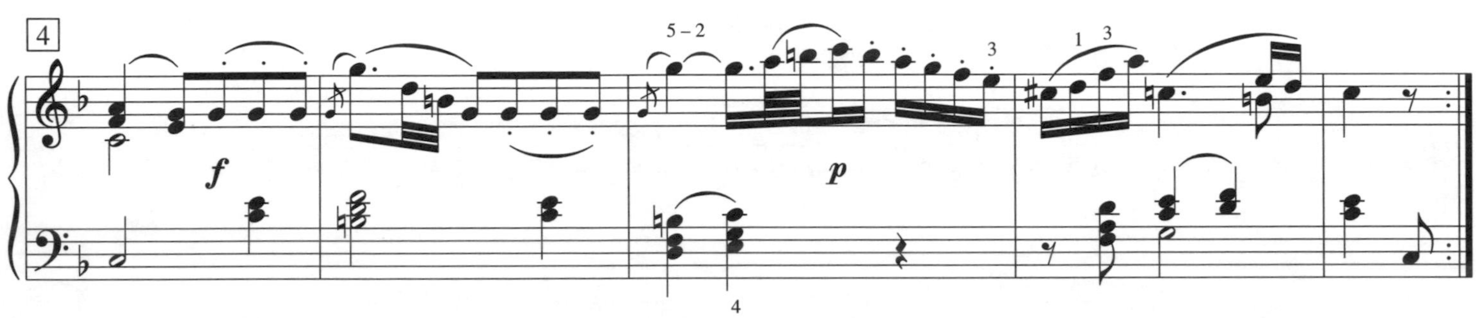

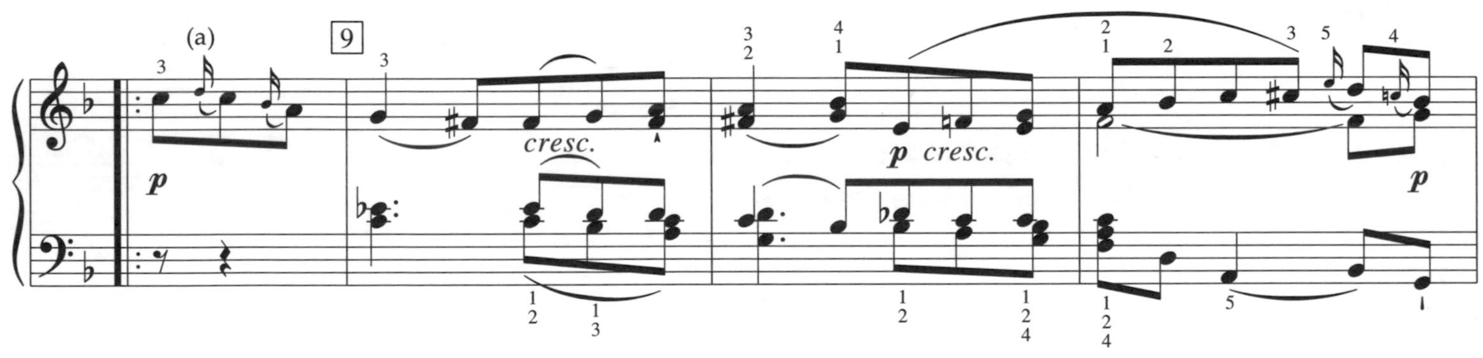

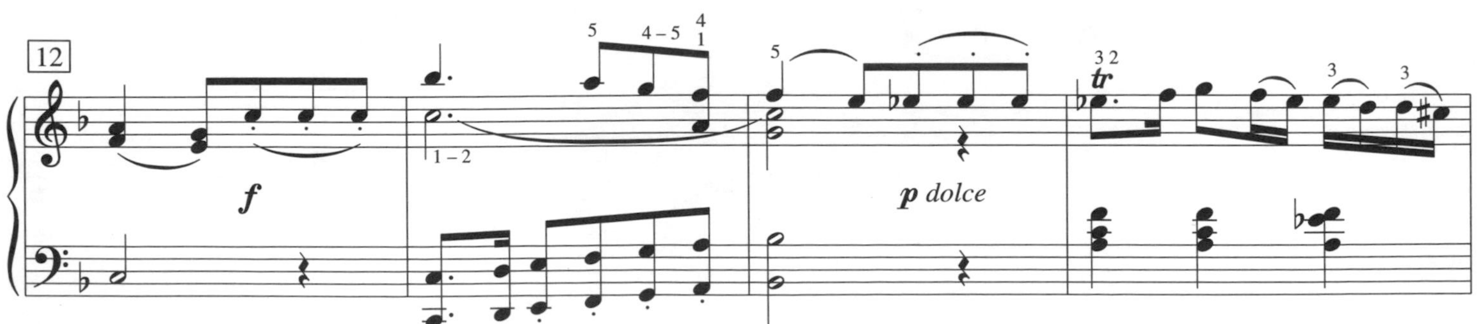

(a) 

Composed 1778
The stroke (▾) indicates *staccato.*

16
cresc.
f
p
21
pp
24
cresc.
f
p
29
f
sf
p
32
cresc.
f
p

37
pp
41
p dolce
f
p
f
46
p
cresc.
50
p cresc.
p
f
p dolce
tr
56
sf
p
cresc.
f
p
60
pp

Sonata in E Minor

Hob. XVI:34

I

Franz Joseph Haydn
(1732 – 1809)

The stroke (ˇ) indicates *staccato*.
For examinations, play only one of the three movements.

II

Adagio ♩ = 48 – 56

The stroke (ꜜ) indicates *staccato*.
For examinations, play only one of the three movements.

17
(b)
tr
21
tr
25
27
29
più adagio
(b)
tr

Tempo I
attacca subito

III

The stroke (▾) indicates *staccato*.
For examinations, play only one of the three movements.

38
44
fz
50
56
63
70

77
82
87
93
98
103

108
fz
tr
113
118
tr
123
128
132
tr

Sonata in G Major

op. 79

I

Ludwig van Beethoven
(1770 – 1827)

Composed 1809

36
cresc.
sf
sf
dim.
cresc.
sf
42
sf
dim.
p
tr
f
p
50
1.
2.
f
f
f
sf
56
sf
sf
sf
62
sf
sf
sf
sf
p
dolce
69

75
f
p
82
cresc.
f
sf
89
p
sf
dolce
96
f
103
p
f
p
cresc.
110
p
dolce

117
cresc.
f
124
sf
131
p leggiermente
138
145
cresc.
sf
p
cresc.
152
sf
p
cresc.

159
sf
sf
dim.
cresc.
sf
sf
dim.
166
p
tr
f
1.
p
f
170
2.
p
f
p
f
177
sf
f
sf
183
f
sf
f
189
sf
p dolce e leggiermente
195

Rondo in C Major

op. 51, no. 1

Ludwig van Beethoven
(1770 – 1827)

18
21
sf
(a)
24
26
sf
sf
29
cresc.
f
p
32
cresc.
decresc.
p
(a)

35
cresc.
39
sfp
sf
decresc.
pp
44
48
tr
Minore
52
sf
54

57
ff
59
p
62
65
cresc.
f
sf
67
sf
sf
70
sf

73
a tempo
calando
p
76
79
sf
82
85
87
cresc.

ff
decresc.
p
sf
tr

rit.
pp
legato
cresc.
f
sfp
f

119
fp
p
122
124
sf
sf
sf
sf
127
p
129
sfp
132
rinf.
rinf.
cresc.
ff

Herberge

The Wayside Inn

op. 82, no. 6

Robert Schumann
(1810 – 1856)

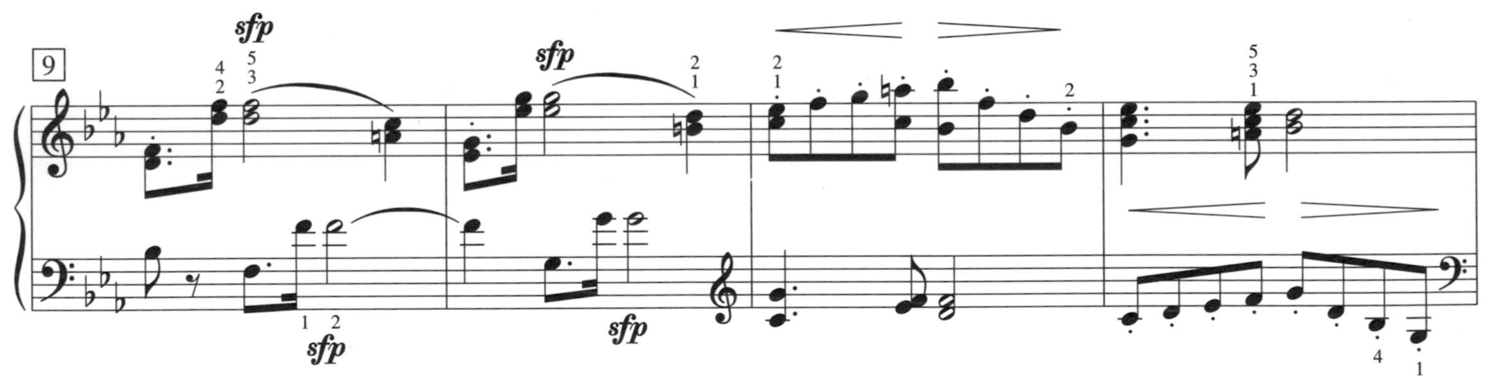

Source: *Waldszenen: neun Klavierstücke,* op. 82 (1848 – 1849)

17
21
etwas zurückhaltend
25
im Tempo
29
33
tr

37
41
45
49
53
etwas zurückhaltend
im Tempo
dim.
ten.
etwas langsamer
im Tempo

Impromptu

op. 142, no. 2

Franz Schubert
(1797 – 1828)

Source: *Vier Impromptus für Klavier*, op. posth. 142, D 935 (1827)

Trio
47
p
simile
51
55
decresc.
pp
59
f
63
cresc.
67
8va
ff
fz
fz
fz

72
fz
fz
fz
fz
p
76
decresc.
tr
81
86
decresc.
pp
91
m.d.
decresc.
96
sempre legato
pp

102
110
f
118
ff
ffz
p
ffz
126
p
pp
pp
134
141
cresc.
rit.
p

Lost Happiness

op. 38, no. 2

Felix Mendelssohn
(1809 – 1847)

Source: *Lieder ohne Worte,* op. 38 (Bonn, 1837)

22
f
26
30
34
p
38
42
cresc.

46
sf
f
50
sf
sf
54
sf
f
sf
58
sf
p
62
cresc.
66
f
dim.
p

Waltz

op. posth. 70, no. 2

Frédéric Chopin
(1810 – 1849)

Source: *Trois valses*, op. posth. 70

26
31
36
42
48
54
dim.

60
f
66
1
tr
1
tr
1
cresc.
5
72
f
mf
1
2
4
cresc.
78
83
f
88
p

93
98
f
p
103
f
dim.
pp
109
p
114
f
119
tr
tr
cresc.

Mazurka

op. posth. 67, no. 4

Frédéric Chopin
(1810 – 1849)

Composed 1846
Source: *Four Mazurkas,* op. posth. 67

f
dolce

Intermezzo

op. 76, no. 7

Johannes Brahms
(1833 – 1897)

Source: *Acht Klavierstücke*, op. 76 (1878)

23
p
27
poco cresc.
p
32
1.
2.
34
dim. e poco rit.
38
mp
p
42
mp

Notturno
op. 54, no. 4

Edvard Grieg
(1843 – 1907)

Source: *Lyrische Stücke,* op. 54 (Leipzig, 1891)

a tempo
15
p
poco
18
p
poco
più mosso
21
pp
ped. una corda
24
ppp
poco a poco cresc.
27
ped. tre corda
molto cresc.
ff
30
poco rit.

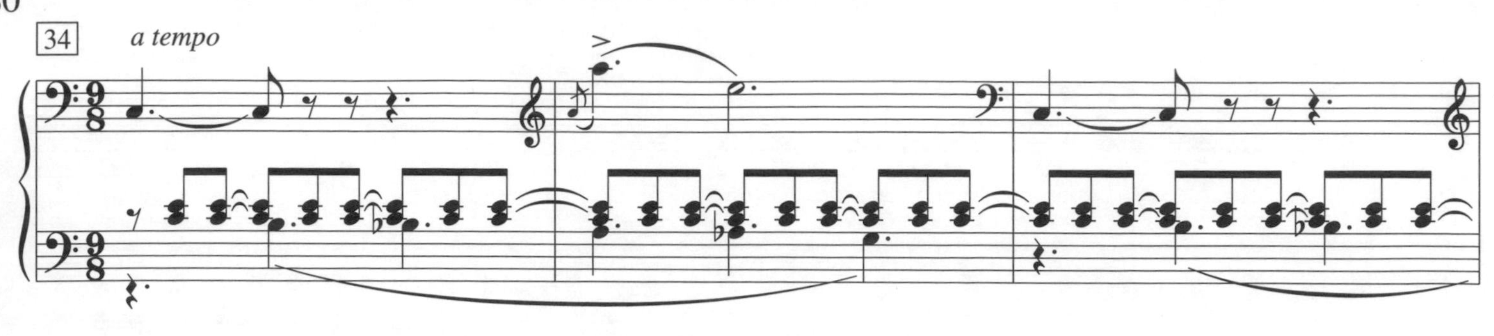
34
a tempo

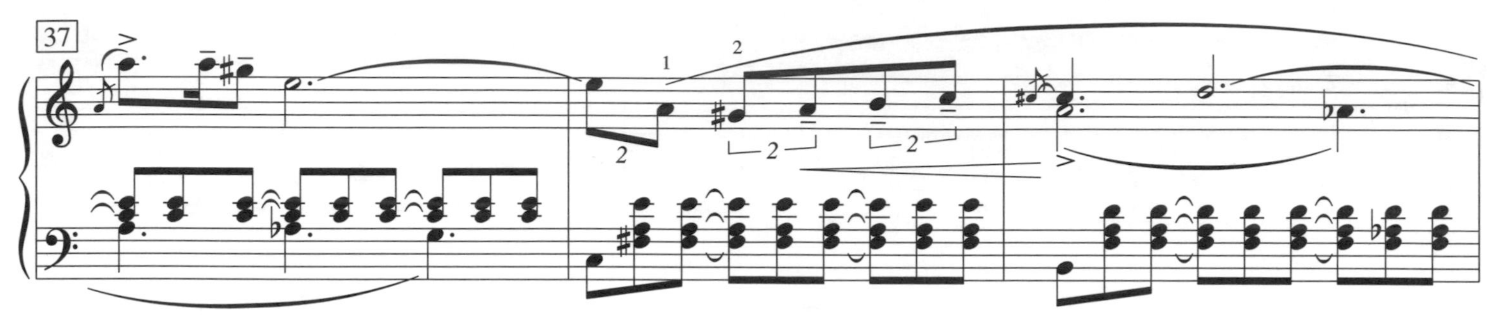
37

40
p
cresc. molto

43
f

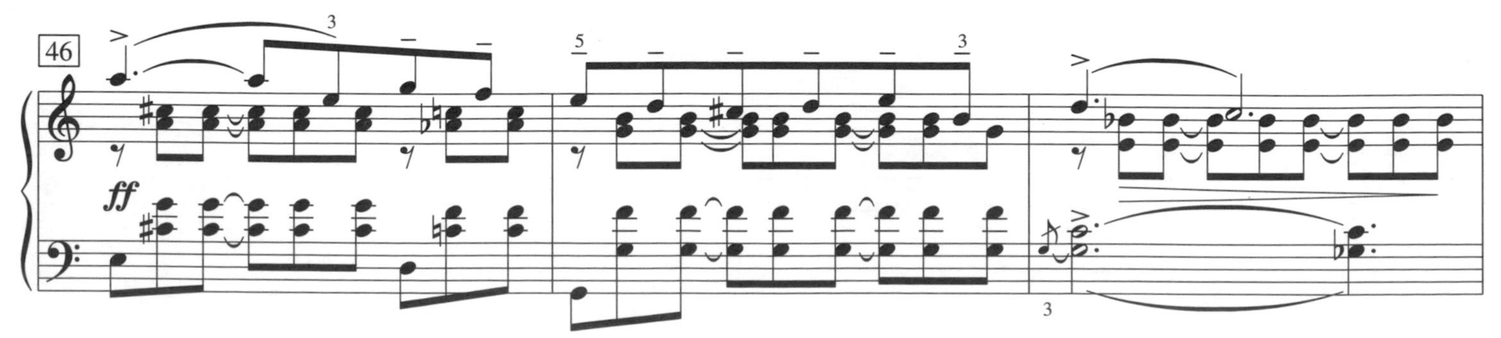
46
ff

49
dim. sempre
52
poco rit.
55
a tempo
p
57
8va
morendo
60
8va
Adagio
pp

June (Barcarole)

op. 37a, no. 6

Pyotr Il'yich Tchaikovsky
(1840 – 1893)

Source: *Die Jahreszeiten: Zwölf Charakterstücke (nach lyrischen Epigraphen),* op. 37a

17
dim.
21
p
25
28
Poco più mosso ♩ = 98
32
p ma poco a poco cresc.
35

L'istesso tempo
f
cresc.
8va
ff
poco riten.
Lento ♩ = 69
f
mf
Tempo I
p

58
61
64
68
72
75
dim.
p

79
p
83
86
89
pp
92
un poco cresc.
96
pp

Sacro-Monte

op. 55, no. 5

Joaquín Turina
(1882 – 1949)

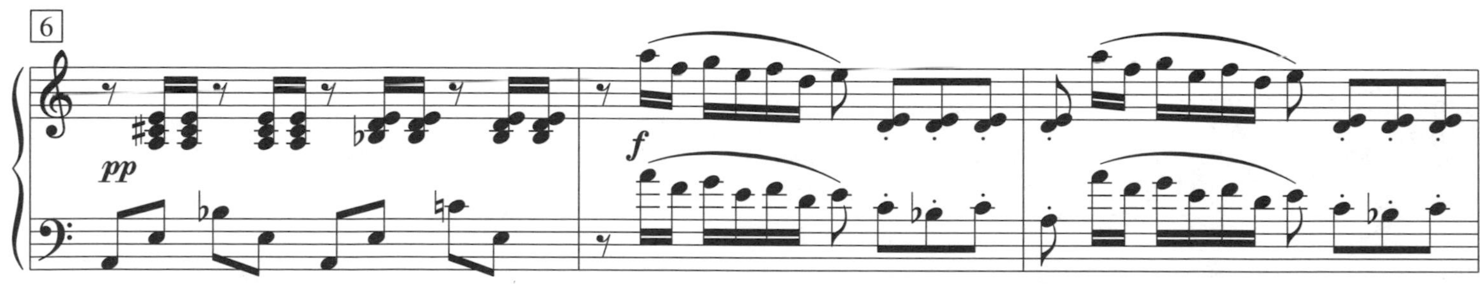

Source: *Cinco danzas gitanas*, op. 55 (1930)

15
sfz
p
8va
18
sfz
p
21
sfz
sfz
8va
24
f
p
8va
27
sfz
dim.
30
p
pp

32
f
1 2 2 5

35
Più vivo ♩ = 120
3
simile
mf

38
f

41
cresc.
ff

44
tr
fff

La fille aux cheveux de lin

Claude Debussy
(1862 – 1918)

Source: *Préludes,* 1er livre (1910)

20
p
mf
Cédez
// Mouvt. (sans lourdeur)
23
p
pp
p
Cédez
// au Mouvt.
très doux
27
pp
Mumuré et en retenant peu à peu
32
pp
35
perdendosi
pp

La sarabande

Ceux qui viendront ici danser
N'auront plus besoin de jambes légères:
Voici votre tour, marquis et bergères,
En fanfreluches du passé.

Les archets aux doigts des musiciens
Pour la sarabande s'attardent assez
Et les souliers fins vont sans se presser
Sur le rythme de cet air ancien.

Une dernière note meurt aux violons
Comme un aveu plus tendre;
Les robes à falbalas sur les hauts talons
Tournent sans plus attendre

Et par couples las,
A pas menus, toute la bande
Des danseurs de sarabande
S'en va.

Tristan Klingsor

Source: *L'almanach aux images; d'après des poèmes de Tristan Klingsor*

15
p
19
8va
sempre legato
p
21
8va
23
26
legato
p
29

32
dim.
rit.
a tempo
ppp
sempre legato
ed espressivo
35
8va
38
41
dim.
ppp
46
pppp
dim.
sempre dim.

Romance

op. 24, no. 9

Jean Sibelius
(1865 – 1957)

Source: *Ten Pieces*, op. 24 (1894 – 1903)

19
f
sfz
sfz
mf
23
f
p
27
sopra
espressivo
p
31
ben marcato
p
mf
con pedale

35
p
senza ped.
p
ben marcato
mf
con pedale
39
mp dolce
p
senza ped.
poco cresc.
43
poco f
47
più f
cresc. molto
con pedale

51
f cresc. possibile
3
4

8va
m.d.
m.s.
53
fz dim. poco

54

55
8va
ten.

56
fz
f
simile
fz
con pedale
60
meno f
con pedale
p
mp dolce
64
67
più p
71
f
mf
mp allargando

Salta, Salta

Termina a grande folia,
e saltando de alegria
recolhem-se, engarupadas,
*nos cavallinhos de páu. **

Octavio Pinto
(1890 – 1950)

* And now playtime is over,
And the children
Come prancing happily home
On their wooden hobby horses.

Source: *Scenas Infantis*

Laughing
Prancing
15
ff
f
19
mf
p
cresc.
Helter-skelter
23
slower
8va
f quicker
simile
26
29
gradually slower
ff
very fast
8va

Variations in D Major

op. 40, no. 1

Dmitri Kabalevsky
(1904 – 1987)

Introduction

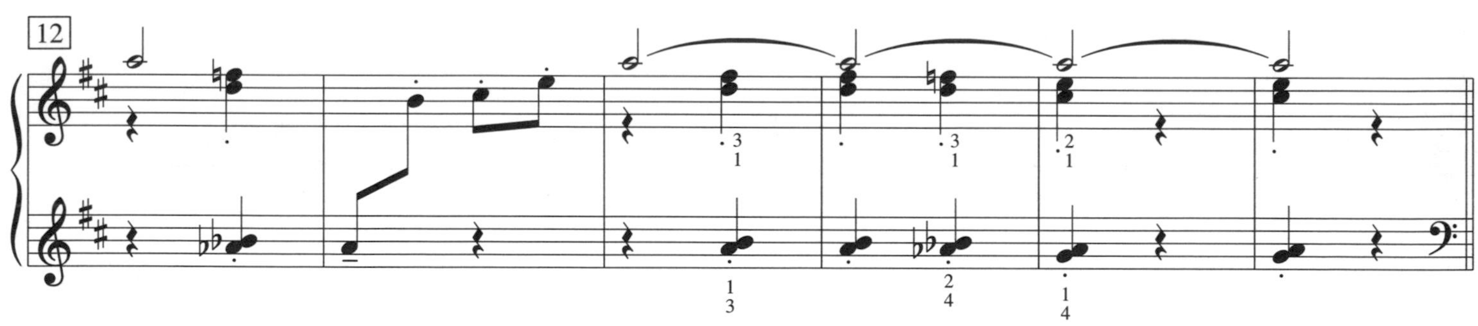

Theme

Source: *Variations for Piano*, op. 40

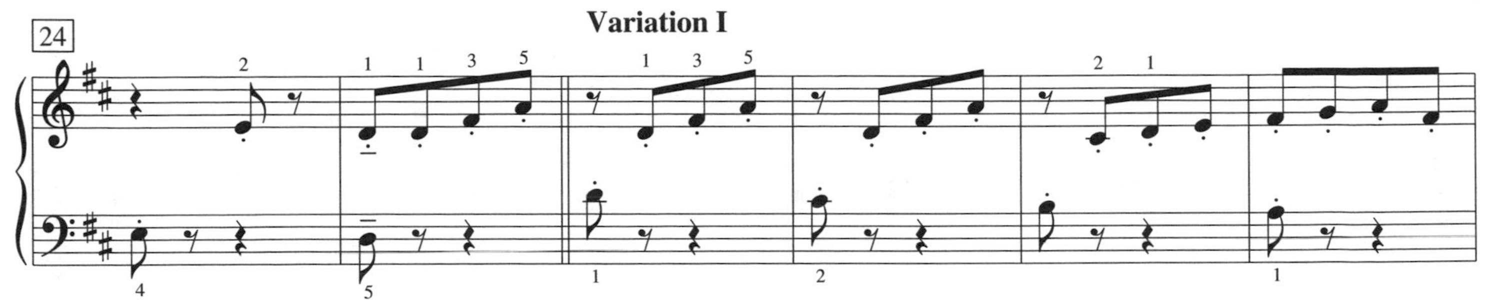

Variation III

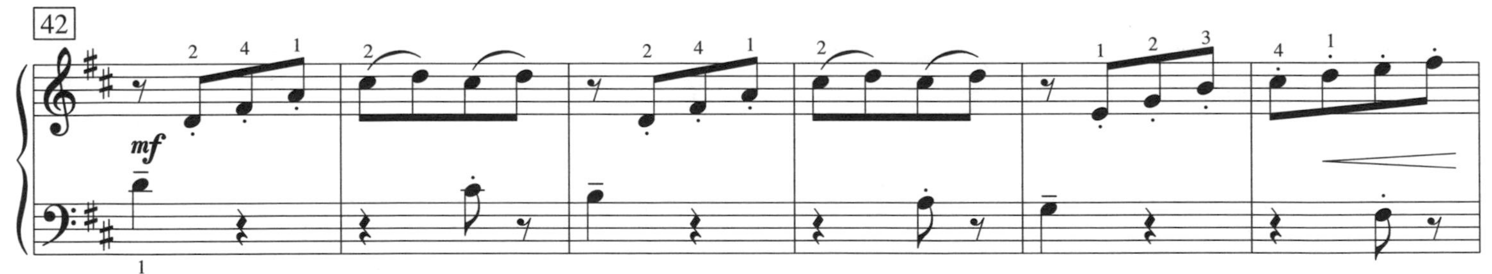

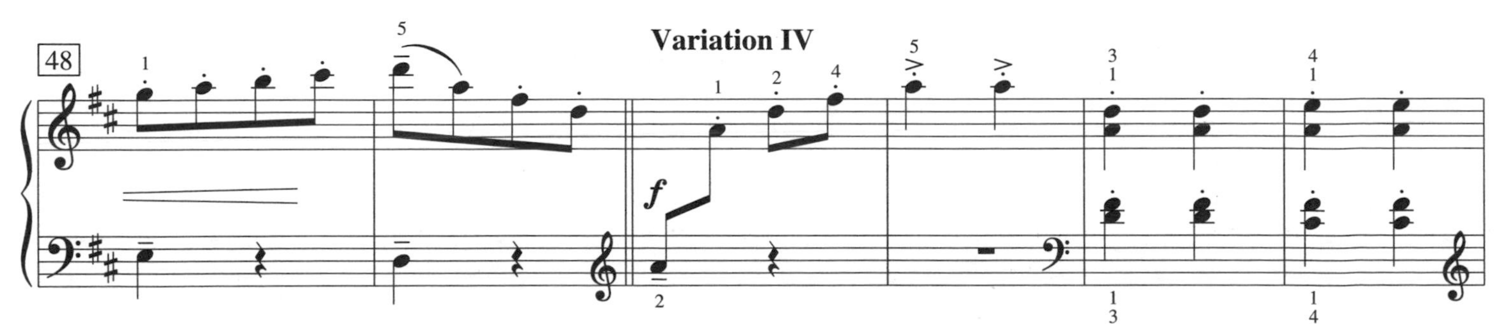

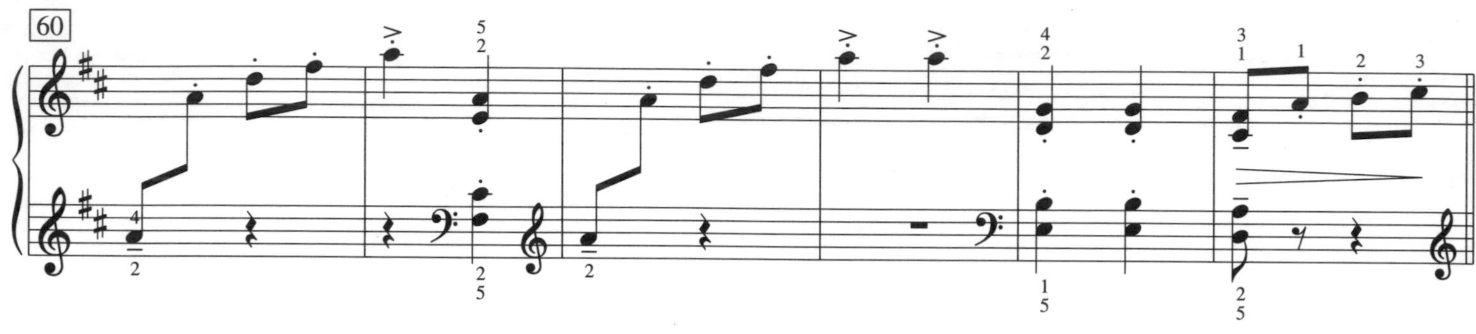

Variation V

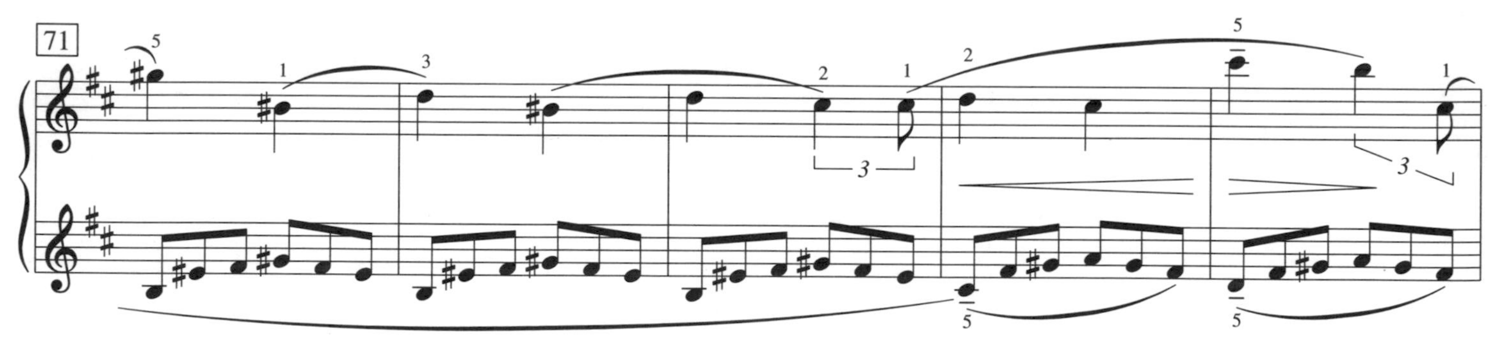

Variation VI
simile
cresc.
Variation VII

Variation VIII

Variation XI
136
mp leggiero
141
146
151
156
Variation XII and Coda
più f

162
166
170
sempre f
175
181
8va
ff

Dance No. 1

Ewart Bartley
(1909 – 1987)

Source: *Two Dances for Piano*

27
mf
sf
32
8va
mf
sf
37
ff
m.s.
m.d.
m.d.
m.s.
mf
42
mp
poco rall.
49
a tempo
f
54
m.d.
m.s.
mp
sost. ped.

59
m.d.
m.s.
m.d.
f
63
ff
68
8va
dim. poco rall.
mp
73
a tempo
ff
mf
78
molto cresc.
ff
mf
83

88

8va

dim.

poco rall.

mp

93 *a tempo*

f

98

103

f

108

113

ff

f

118
mp
123
sos. ped.
f
128
1
2
1
ff
133
138
mf
mp
144
p
mf
mp

Distant Memories

Alexina Louie
(1949 –)

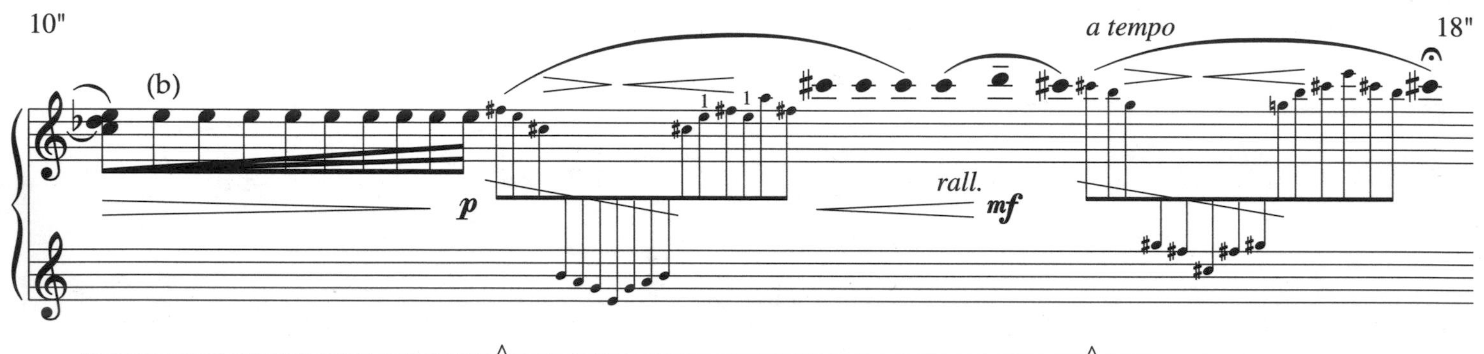

N.B.: Accidentals in the *senza misura* sections apply only to the note that they precede; repeated notes are all governed by the accidental preceding the first note of the group.

(a) *Una corda* may be used.

(b) The number of repeated notes is left to the discretion of the performer; the notes may be divided between the hands.

Source: *Music for Piano* (1982)

7
rit.
Più mosso ♩ = 80
10
p
mf
p
14
mf
mf
p
18
mf

22
a tempo
p
poco rit.

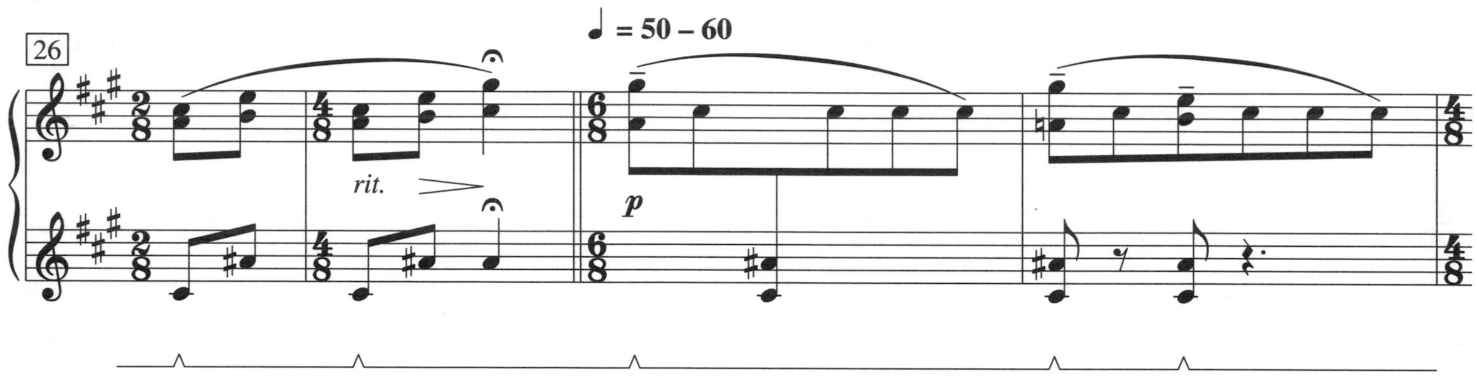
26
♩ = 50 – 60
rit.
p

30

33
rit.

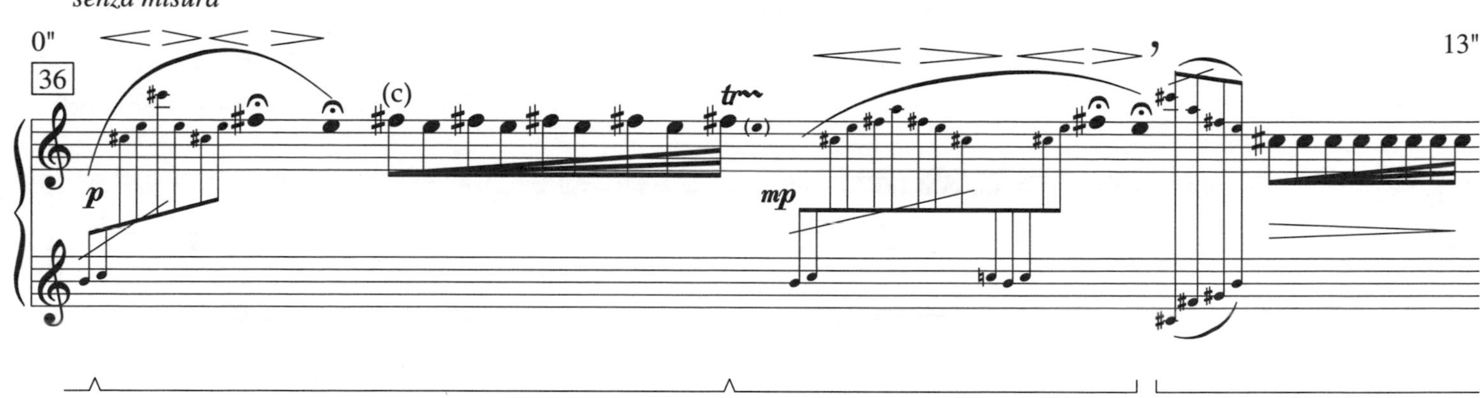

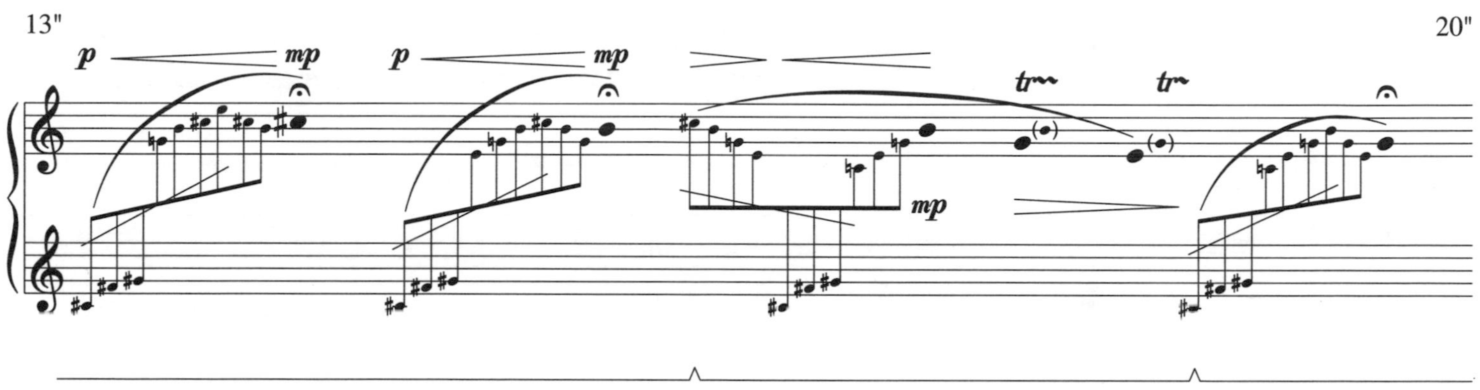

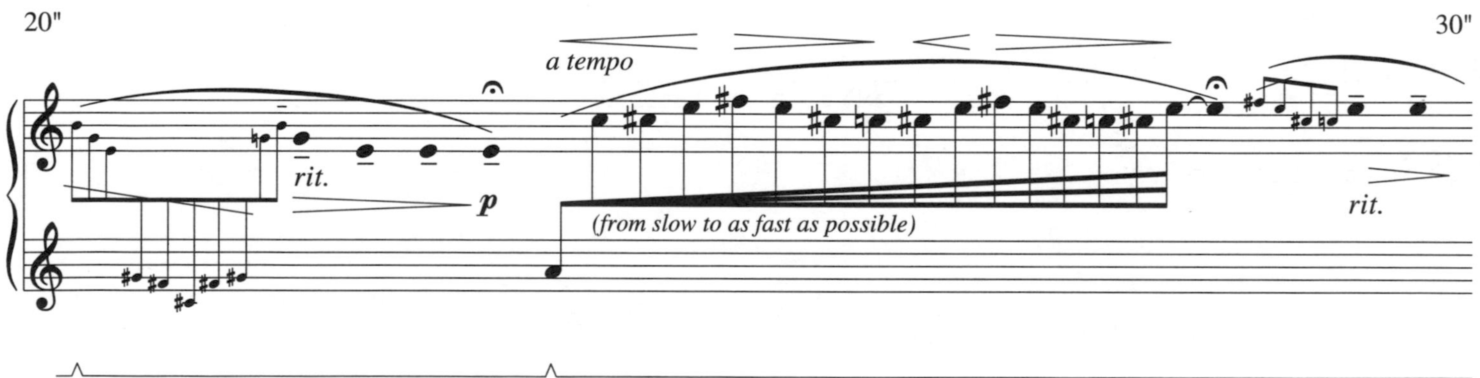

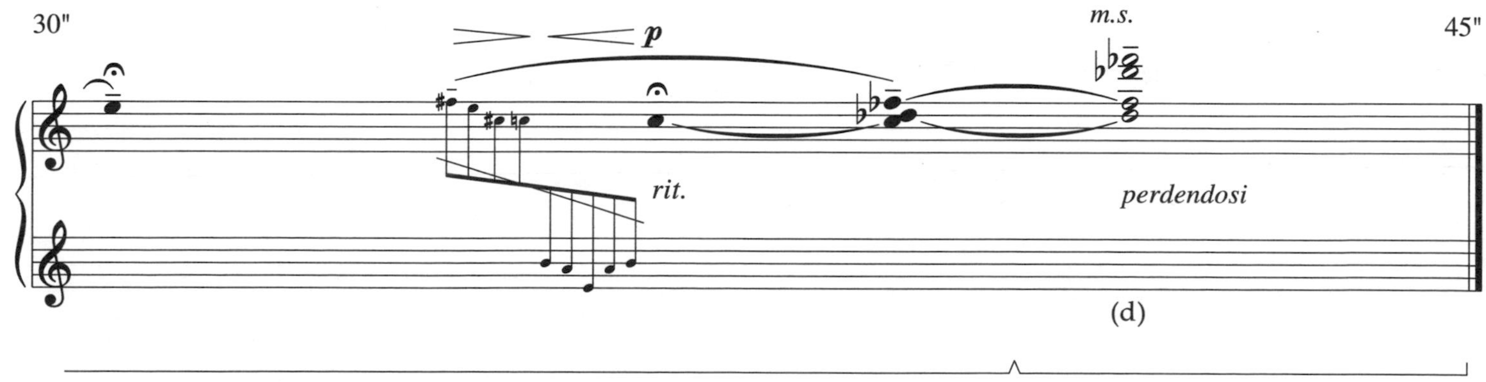

(c) The number of notes leading to the trill and the number of repeated notes are left to the discretion of the performer; the repeated notes may be divided between the hands.

(d) Only the D flats and the F flats should sound through the pedal change.

Humoreske

Rodin Konstantinovich Shchedrin
(1932 –)

Composed 1957

Source: *Piano Pieces*

16
mf
19
p sub.
senza ped.
sff
21
8va
pp
24
sf
p
27
sff
sff
mp

30
5 1
4 1
3 1
f
mp
8va
36
ff
8va
distinto espressivo
39
pp
senza ped.
42
sff
45
p
pp

49
f
mf
p sub.
senza ped.
52
8va
sf
p
morendo poco a poco
55
mf
p
pp
58
sf
61
p secco
8va
pp
poco rit.
8va
sfff

Over the Rainbow

Harold Arlen
(1904 – 1986)
arr. George Shearing

Source: *The Wizard of Oz* (1939), words by Edgar Yipsel Harburg (1898 – 1981); arrangement from *The Genius of George Shearing: Piano Solos*

19
sempre stacc.
22
25
mf
28
31
mp
34
rit. e dim.

Le nez
The Nose

Clermont Pépin
(1926 –)

After a tale by Nicolas Gogol: a nose, having escaped from its master, parades around town in a general's uniform.

Source: *Trois petites pièces pour piano / Pièces faciles pour piano* (1953)

15
f
m.d.
19
p
23
mf
27
f
31

35
pp
1
5
2
1
2
3
2
1
3
1

39
p

43

46
rit.
a tempo
3
1
4
2
5
1
3
1
5
2
2
5
1
2
2
4